THE DECISION DASHBOARD

Run your business
from ONE sheet of paper

CLAIRE CHANDLER

ALSO BY CLAIRE CHANDLER

The Whirlpool Effect:
Inspire the FLOW that Boosts Company Performance

Leading Beyond A Crisis:
A Conversation About What's Next
(co-authored with Ben Baker)

Chicks with Sticks:
How to Handle Your Business on the Golf Course

Visit www.ClaireChandler.net\books for more details.

CONTENTS

ABOUT THE DECISION DASHBOARD
The One Page That Drives Greater Business Success

The rate of leadership failure is downright scary. Based on their research, most experts say that at least 50% of all new senior-level and executive leaders fail within 18 months... and that the cost of that failure can climb as high as 20 times that leader's annual compensation.

I've done my own research as well. Recently, I invited over 300 human resources executives and 100 newly transitioned leaders to have a conversation with me about their experiences. Those conversations revealed three primary reasons why leaders underperform—or outright fail:

1. Lack of preparedness;
2. Lack of mission clarity; and
3. Indecisiveness.

The Decision Dashboard solves all 3 of these leadership land mines.

While this book has several pages, the end result of following these steps will be a ONE-PAGE Decision Dashboard that you can carry around with you.

When you build this Decision Dashboard, you WILL increase your probability of success AND accelerate the performance of your teams

So take time to build your dashboard. Your decisions will become better, faster and easier. Your team's performance will accelerate. And your role as a leader will be more fulfilling.

To your success,
Claire Chandler

Chapter 1

BE PREPARED

Chapter 1
BE PREPARED

STAKEHOLDER MAP

Whether you are new to your leadership role or you have been in the seat awhile, it's important to identify the stakeholders, in all directions, who have authority and/or influence over your role and, consequently, your success. These stakeholders include your direct manager, your direct reports, key client and/or customer contacts... anyone you need to get to know and build rapport with to succeed in your role.

Fill in the table at the end of this chapter with as many key stakeholders as you can think of:

- What is their name and role?

- Are they internal or external to your organization?

- What is their current level of INTEREST in (i.e. support of or opposition to) your role, team and/or company? Use a simple 3-point rating scale, such as low/medium/high or red/yellow/green.

- What is their current level of IMPACT on (i.e. ability to help or hinder) the success of your role, team and/or company? Use the same 3-point rating scale as above.

LISTENING TOUR

One of the biggest regrets new leaders shared was not talking to more people SOONER in their role and building relationships with their key stakeholders. The most successful leaders go on a personal "listening tour"—ideally within their first 60 days—to learn more about their key stakeholders and how they can partner with them.

As you meet with each of these stakeholders, fill in the rest of your stakeholder map at the end of this chapter:

- What do they expect / need from you?
- What do you need from them?
- How do they prefer to communicate?
- What do they value, i.e. what is most important to them?

It's important to ask your stakeholders for their input so they feel heard, understood, and included—and less inclined to create roadblocks. Their answers will help you to gather insights and crystallize your mission, so be sure to listen intently.

YOUR STAKEHOLDERS

NAME	ROLE	I/E	INTEREST	IMPACT	THEIR NEEDS	YOUR NEEDS	COMMUNIC ATION	VALUES/ GOALS

Chapter 2

BE CLEAR

Chapter 2
BE CLEAR

YOUR MISSION

There are a surprising number of leaders who jump feet first into a new role without completing two critical activities:

1. Clearly articulating and understanding their mission.

2. Ensuring they and their direct manager are in complete alignment on the mission.

Lack of mission clarity and alignment elongate the learning curve. So don't skip this step. Your mission is **foundational** to the success of your team and of you as their leader.

Your direct manager may take for granted that you will know exactly what you're supposed to accomplish. OR they may not be completely clear on the mission themselves. So it's essential that you synthesize all the input you gathered during your listening tour; calibrate it through discussions with your direct manager; and articulate your mission clearly and consistently. After all, if you can't convey to your team what you're striving to accomplish, how will you ever get there... or even realize when you've reached your destination?

Think of your mission as your purpose or your "Point B": Why does your role exist? What was your team put in place to accomplish? What is the end goal?

Write a clear, concise statement of your MISSION in the space below.

_____

_____

_____

_____

_____

_____

_____

YOUR MISSION-CRITICAL DNA

Now that you clearly understand your mission or "Point B"—i.e., your desired future state—what will it take to get there?

Start by identifying your mission-critical DNA.

What fundamental capabilities, skills, technical expertise, knowledge and behaviors will you and your team need to possess and demonstrate to achieve your mission?

Using the table on the following page, compile as comprehensive a list as possible of your mission-critical attributes.

Once you have a fairly complete list, rate your team's current competency, on a scale from 1-10—1 being a significant weakness, gap or deficiency; and 10 being a clear, deep, demonstrable strength.

MISSION-CRITICAL DNA

ATTRIBUTE	CURRENT COMPETENCY

YOUR FLOW CHART

Now we're ready to build your Decision Dashboard, using the FLOW chart method.

MISSION: Take the mission you wrote on page 6. Tweak it if necessary; then rewrite it in the MISSION box on your Decision Dashboard, which is the last page of this book. Then fill in the remaining boxes as follows:

FUNDAMENTALS

Review your list of mission-critical attributes on page 8. Any attributes rated 6 or lower are currently Fundamental gaps. Write those items in the FUNDAMENTALS box on your Decision Dashboard.

LEVERS

The attributes on page 8 rated higher than 6 are current strengths. These are competitive advantages that you and your team can Leverage. Write those items in the LEVERS box on your Decision Dashboard.

OBSTACLES

What Obstacles stand in the way of your ability to achieve your mission? Write those in the OBSTACLES box on your Decision Dashboard.

WINS

What will success look like? How will you know a Win when you see it? What milestones must you hit? What Quick Wins can you implement? Write those in the WINS box on your Decision Dashboard.

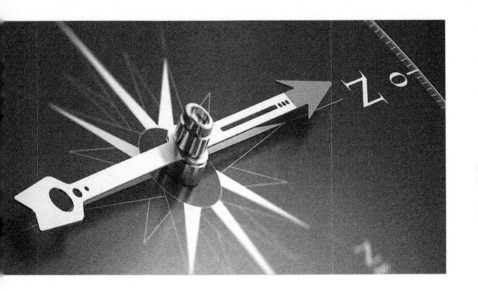

Chapter 3

BE DECISIVE

Chapter 3
BE DECISIVE

RUN YOUR BUSINESS FROM ONE PAGE

The leaders I work with literally walk around with this one-page Decision Dashboard in their pocket. Whenever they need to make a decision--whether strategic or day-to-day--they measure it against the dashboard and ask, Does this decision:

- Address one of our Fundamental gaps?

- Leverage one of our competitive strengths?

- Minimize or eliminate an Obstacle?

- Move us closer to a Win?

Once you complete your own Decision Dashboard, carry it around with you and refer to it as often as possible.

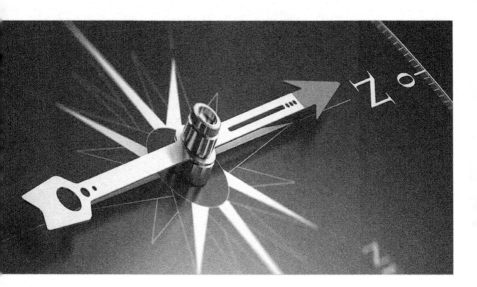

Chapter 4

SO... NOW WHAT?

Chapter 4
SO... NOW WHAT?

MAXIMIZE YOUR ROI

If you've reached this point in the book, you've invested a good amount of time and effort in building your Decision Dashboard. Well done! Now make sure you maximize your return on that investment.

Repeat this process every time you take on a new role, experience a significant pivot in your business, undertake a new project or strategic initiative... any time you have a new mission. Whether leading a new team, a new project, or a new strategy, this one-page Decision Dashboard will enable you to make better, faster and easier decisions—whether those decisions are long-term or day-to-day.

Also, don't complete this dashboard process in a vacuum. Use the opportunity to solicit input and build buy-in. Ask your team, especially your key stakeholders, for their feedback as you complete each step.

Here are a few more ways you can use this Decision Dashboard to run your business:

- **Change your communication from reactive to strategic.** Using the Decision Dashboard as a guide, connect everything you do to your team's mission and to how their individual talents, efforts and ideas contribute to that mission.

- **Increase your team's skills and capabilities.** Focus every dollar you invest in training on increasing their competency in one or more of your Fundamentals. Every new person you hire onto your team should possess a natural talent in one of your Fundamental gaps and complement your existing Levers of strength.

- **Eliminate roadblocks and accelerate performance.** The more you rely on your Decision Dashboard, the easier your conversations with your team will become. You will be better able to resolve conflict, correct behavior, provide feedback, and motivate higher levels of performance by conveying clearer expectations: Your people's performance and behavior either ADVANCE you toward your mission or pull you farther away from it. It will become easier and easier to demonstrate the difference and manage to those expectations.

THE BOTTOM LINE

The most successful leaders are those who are:

- Well prepared for their role;

- Crystal-clear on their mission and their expectations; and

- Decisive—on both day-to-day and long-term issues.

When you incorporate this Decision Dashboard into your strategy, you will join their ranks.

Chapter 5

AN INVITATION

Chapter 5
AN INVITATION

ACCELERATE YOUR PERFORMANCE

In all my interviews with business leaders, one theme was constant:

Leaders don't need training. They need results.

When leaders have access to a sounding board, they significantly flatten their ramp to full confidence. They are far more likely to ask for help, admit when they don't know something, and open themselves up to feedback if they can talk through their challenges and ideas with someone with the objectivity, expertise and perspective to help them navigate their business landscape.

Business leaders turn to me for many reasons. But here are the biggies:

- I get results.

- I help my clients breathe easier.

- Despite my background in HR, I don't talk like someone from HR. And THAT's why my clients listen to me.

If you'd like to explore what's possible when you have someone you can turn to, I'd like to extend a special invitation.

Sign up for a free 30-minute sounding board with me.

We'll define your Point B and the biggest obstacle standing in your way. If we agree that we're a mutual fit, we'll discuss how we can work together to design and execute the game plan you need to achieve your mission.

To sign up, visit
www.ClaireChandler.net/Talk-to-Claire
and book a 30-minute Sounding Board appointment.

Chapter 6

YOUR DECISION DASHBOARD

Chapter 6
YOUR DECISION DASHBOARD

RUN YOUR BUSINESS FROM ONE SHEET OF PAPER

Build your one-page Decision Dashboard. Carry it with you. And never struggle to make a business decision again.

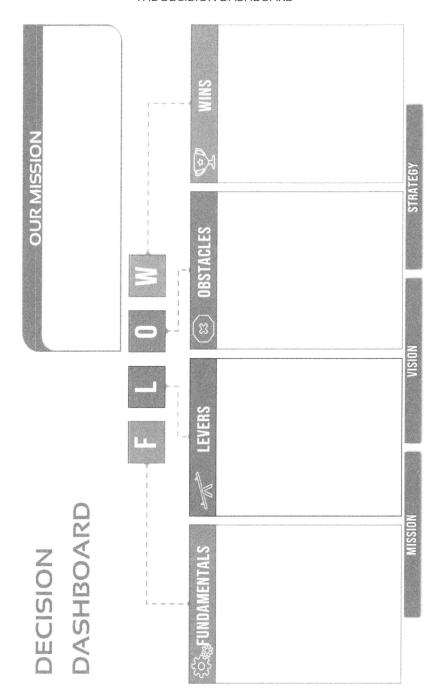

Printed in Great Britain
by Amazon

24636284R00030